W9-CMO-363

CELEBRATING HOLIDAYS

Holi

by Rachel Grack

BELLWETHER MEDIA • MINNEAPOLIS, MN

Note to Librarians, Teachers, and Parents:

Blastoff! Readers are carefully developed by literacy experts and combine standards-based content with developmentally appropriate text.

Level 1 provides the most support through repetition of high-frequency words, light text, predictable sentence patterns, and strong visual support.

Level 2 offers early readers a bit more challenge through varied simple sentences, increased text load, and less repetition of high-frequency words.

Level 3 advances early-fluent readers toward fluency through increased text and concept load, less reliance on visuals, longer sentences, and more literary language.

Level 4 builds reading stamina by providing more text per page, increased use of punctuation, greater variation in sentence patterns, and increasingly challenging vocabulary.

Level 5 encourages children to move from "learning to read" to "reading to learn" by providing even more text, varied writing styles, and less familiar topics.

Whichever book is right for your reader, Blastoff! Readers are the perfect books to build confidence and encourage a love of reading that will last a lifetime!

This edition first published in 2019 by Bellwether Media, Inc.

No part of this publication may be reproduced in whole or in part without written permission of the publisher. For information regarding permission, write to Bellwether Media, Inc., Attention: Permissions Department, 6012 Blue Circle Drive, Minnetonka, MN 55343.

Library of Congress Cataloging-in-Publication Data

LC record for Holi available at https://lccn.loc.gov/2017056564

Text copyright © 2019 by Bellwether Media, Inc. BLASTOFF! READERS and associated logos are trademarks and/or registered trademarks of Bellwether Media, Inc. SCHOLASTIC, CHILDREN'S PRESS, and associated logos are trademarks and/or registered trademarks of Scholastic Inc., 557 Broadway, New York, NY 10012.

Editor: Paige Polinsky   Designer: Andrea Schneider

Printed in the United States of America, North Mankato, MN.

Table of Contents

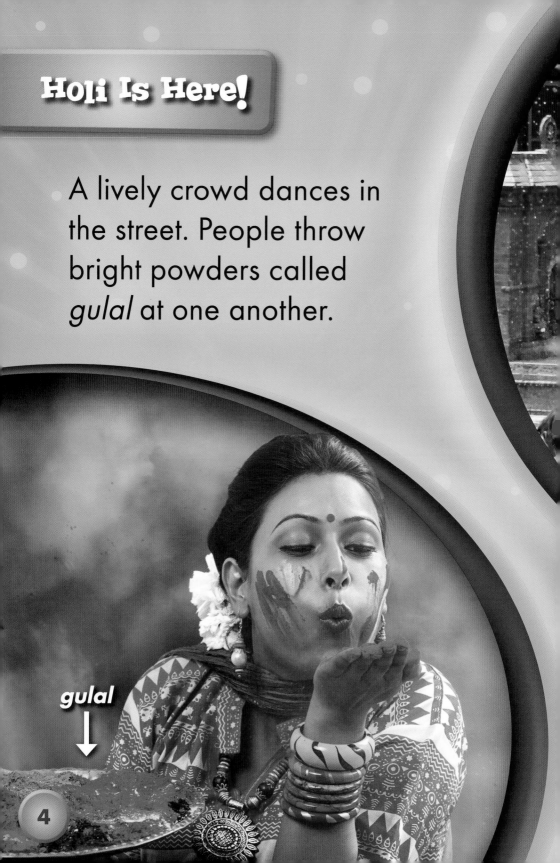

Holi Is Here!

A lively crowd dances in the street. People throw bright powders called *gulal* at one another.

gulal

↓

Clouds of color fill the air.
It is Holi!

Holi, or the **Festival** of Colors, is a joyful holiday in South Asia.

People welcome a bright spring. They celebrate good winning against evil.

How Do You Say?

Word	Pronunciation
gulal	goo-LAHL
gujiya	goo-JEE-uh
Holi	HO-lee
Rigveda	rig-VAY-duh
Vishnu	VISH-noo
Krishna	KRISH-nuh

Who Celebrates Holi?

Holi is a **Hindu** festival.
But others can enjoy it, too.

People forget their **differences** and show love to all.

Holi Beginnings

harvesting

Holi began as a **harvest** festival in India.

Its **traditions** honored Hindu **gods** such as Krishna and Vishnu.

India

N

W E

S

Krishna

Young Krishna was known for playing pranks. He splashed girls with colored water.

Krishna

Vishnu

Vishnu saved a prince. He stopped the **demon** Holika from killing the prince with fire.

13

Time to Celebrate

Holi lasts two days in February or March. It follows the Hindu calendar.

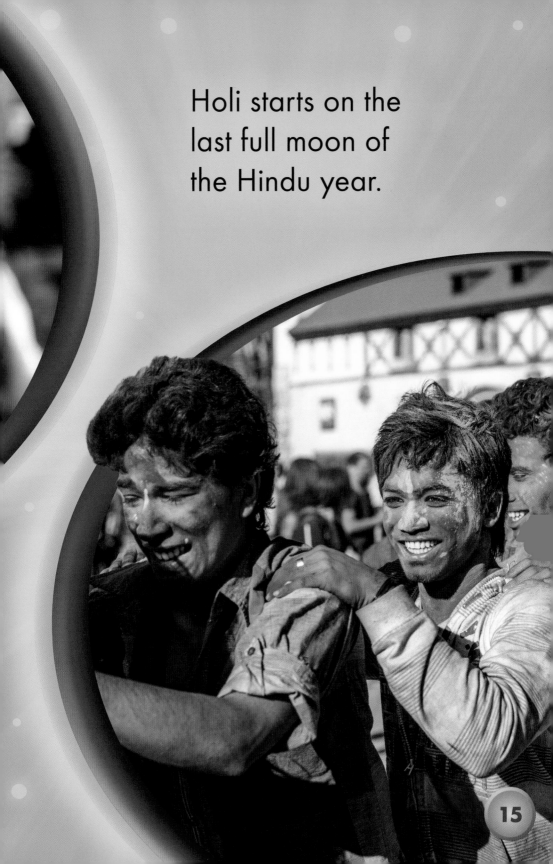

Holi starts on the last full moon of the Hindu year.

15

People light bonfires the night before Holi. They **chant** from the **Rigveda**.

The fire honors Vishnu
for saving the prince.

The next day, people celebrate
Krishna's pranks. They splash
each other with **dyed** water.
Many wear white clothes so
the colors show.

Make Holi Dancers

People dance to joyful music on Holi. Celebrate with your own colorful string of dancers!

What You Need:

- white construction paper
- pencil
- spray bottles
- water
- food coloring
- newspapers
- scissors
- paper punch
- yarn

What You Do:

1. Draw outlines of five to ten people on the paper as shown.
2. Fill the spray bottles halfway with water. Add several drops of food coloring to the bottles. Use a different color for each bottle.
3. Set the paper on the newspapers. Spray the people lightly with colored water. Let dry.
4. Cut the people out. Punch a hole in the top of each head.
5. Thread the yarn through each paper person. Leave some space between them.
6. Tie a knot at each end of the yarn.

Families share tasty treats on Holi. Coconut **dumplings** called *gujiya* are popular.

gujiya

The sounds of music and laughter fill the air. Colorful springtime has begun!

Glossary

chant—to say or sing words or phrases over and over

demon—an evil spirit

differences—the ways things are not alike, such as age and gender

dumplings—an Indian food made of dough wrappers stuffed with meat, vegetables, or sweet filling; dumplings are steamed, fried, or boiled.

dyed—stained or colored

festival—a celebration

gods—holy and supernatural beings

harvest—a time to gather crops

Hindu—related to Hinduism, a religion practiced in India and other parts of the world

Rigveda—the oldest of the holy books of the Hindu religion

traditions—customs, ideas, and beliefs handed down from one generation to the next

To Learn More

AT THE LIBRARY

Grack, Rachel. *Diwali*. Minneapolis, Minn.: Bellwether Media, 2017.

Murphy, Charles. *Celebrations Around the World*. New York, N.Y.: Gareth Stevens Publishing, 2017.

Sehgal, Surishtha, and Kabir Sehgal. *Festival of Colors*. New York, N.Y.: Beach Lane Books, 2018.

ON THE WEB

Learning more about Holi is as easy as 1, 2, 3.

1. Go to www.factsurfer.com.

2. Enter "Holi" into the search box.

3. Click the "Surf" button and you will see a list of related web sites.

With factsurfer.com, finding more information is just a click away.

Index

The images in this book are reproduced through the courtesy of: OHishiapply, front cover; India Picture, p. 4; Kristin Ruhs, pp. 4-5; SatpalSingh, pp. 6-7; v.s.anandhakrishna, pp. 7, 22; david pearson/ Alamy, p. 8; Evgeny Bendin, pp. 8-9; Rawpixel.com, p. 10; Dipak Shelare, p. 11; Dinodia Photos/ Alamy, p. 12; reddees, pp. 12-13; Rudra Narayan Mitra, pp. 14-15; sergemi, p. 15; Tim Graham/ Alamy, p. 16; Paul Brown/ Alamy, pp. 16-17; Krothapalli Ravindra, p. 18; Andrea Schneider/ Bellwether Media, p. 19 (all); RS STOCK IMAGES, p. 20; Johnny Adolphson, pp. 20-21.